UNDERSTAND YOUR Mind AND Body

Asthma

Sarah Harvey

Explore other books at:
WWW.ENGAGEBOOKS.COM

VANCOUVER, B.C.

𝑒 WWW.ENGAGEBOOKS.COM

Asthma: Understand Your Mind and Body
Harvey, Sarah 1950 -
Text © 2023 Engage Books
Design © 2023 Engage Books

Edited by: A.R. Roumanis, Ashley Lee,
Melody Sun, and and Sarah Harvey
Design by: Mandy Christiansen

Text set in Montserrat Regular.
Chapter headings set in Hobgoblin.

FIRST EDITION / FIRST PRINTING

This book is not meant to replace the advice of a medical professional or be a tool for diagnosis. It is an educational tool to help children understand what they or other people are going through.

LIBRARY AND ARCHIVES CANADA CATALOGUING IN PUBLICATION

Title: Asthma / Sarah Harvey.
Names: Harvey, Sarah N., 1950- author.
Description: Series statement: Understand your mind and body

Identifiers: Canadiana (print) 20230165257 | Canadiana (ebook) 20230165265
ISBN 978-1-77476-871-6 (hardcover)
ISBN 978-1-77476-872-3 (softcover)
ISBN 978-1-77476-873-0 (epub)
ISBN 978-1-77476-874-7 (pdf)
ISBN 978-1-77878-107-0 (audio)

Subjects:
LCSH: Asthma in children—Juvenile literature.
LCSH: Asthma—Treatment—Juvenile literature.
LCSH: Asthma—Juvenile literature.

Classification: LCC RJ436.A8 H37 2023 | DDC J618.92/238—DC23

This project has been made possible in part by the Government of Canada.

Canada

Contents

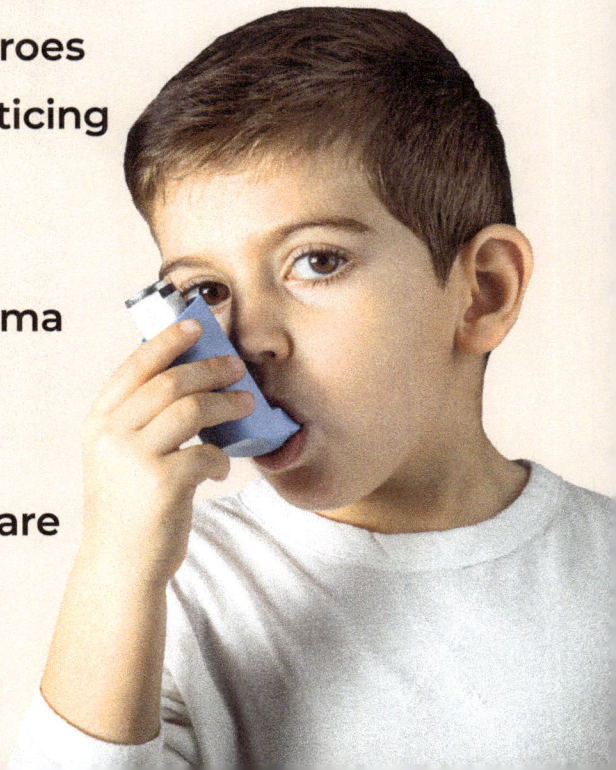

What Is Asthma?

Asthma is a condition that makes it hard to breathe. When people have asthma, their airways may get bigger or tighten. Airways are how air gets in and out of the **lungs**. A lot of thick liquid called mucus is created in the lungs when someone has asthma.

KEY WORD

Lungs: bag-like body parts that are used for breathing.

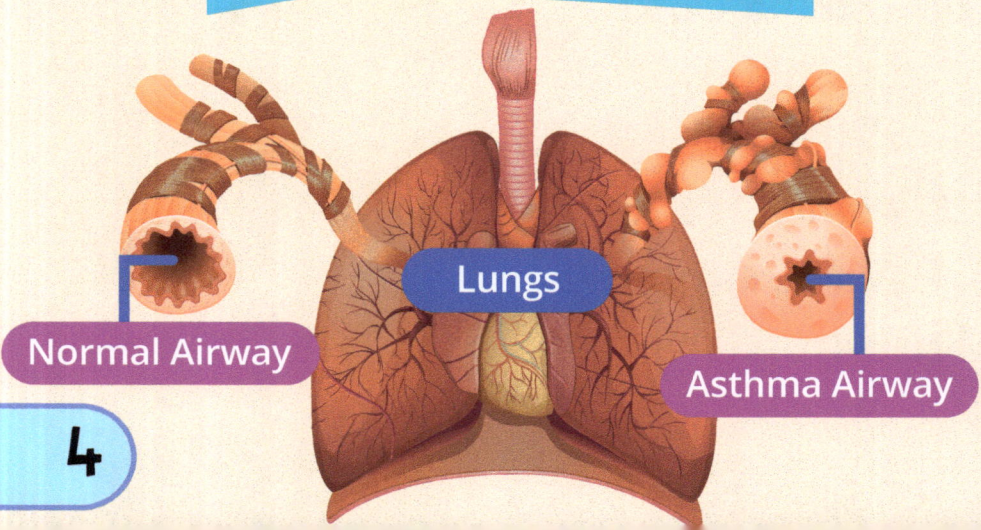

Lungs

Normal Airway

Asthma Airway

Asthma is a very common **chronic** disease. People cannot catch it like a cold. Most childhood asthma starts before age five. Adult asthma can start anytime.

KEY WORD

Chronic: something that lasts for a long time.

Older people often do not know they have asthma so they do not get help.

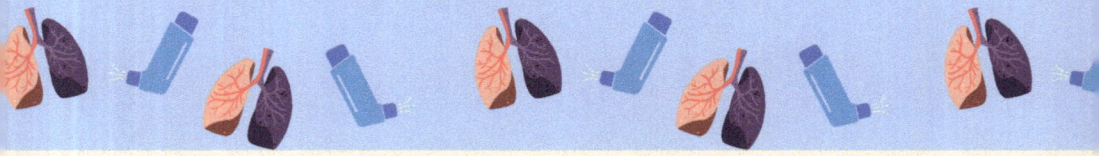

What Causes Asthma?

There is no one simple reason why some people have asthma. It can be passed from a parent to their child. A child is three times more likely than the average child to get asthma if their mother has asthma.

Asthma can also be caused by triggers. Triggers are things that bother a person's airways. Different people have different triggers. Some common triggers are pet hair, air pollution, **pollen**, cold air, and smoke.

KEY WORD

Pollen: a fine powder made by some plants.

Getting a cold or the flu can trigger asthma as well.

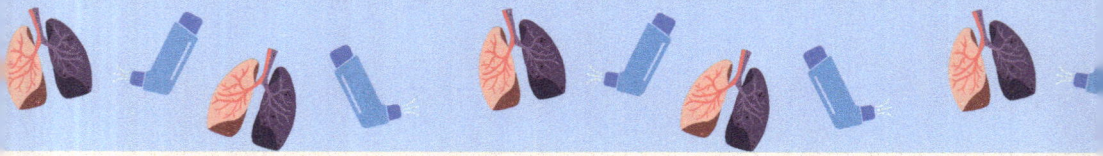

How Does Asthma Affect Your Body?

Asthma affects people's bodies in different ways. Common **symptoms** are shortness of breath, coughing, and wheezing. Chest tightness or pain are also likely.

KEY WORD

Symptoms: something felt in the body that is a sign of illness.

Some people have these symptoms all the time. Others only have symptoms once in a while. Asthma symptoms can come on fast. This is called an asthma attack or episode.

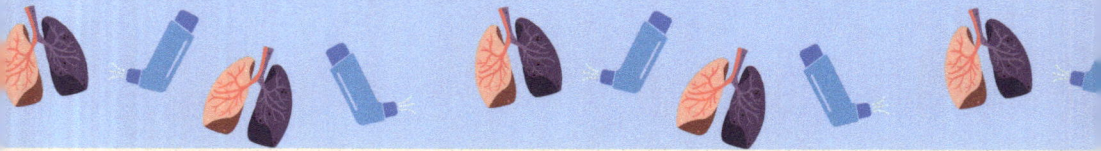

How Does Asthma Affect Your Mind?

The symptoms of asthma can be scary, especially the first time they happen. When someone feels as if they cannot breathe, they may be frightened. People with asthma may worry something is going to trigger their asthma attack. This may lead to **anxiety**.

KEY WORD

Anxiety: feelings of worry and fear that are hard to control.

People with asthma have to avoid certain triggers. This may limit what they can do. They might not be able to do certain activities. They might not be able to hang out with their friends as often as they want to. This may cause a mental illness like **depression**.

KEY WORD

Depression: strong feelings of sadness and lack of hope.

Does Asthma Go Away?

Children with asthma may have fewer symptoms as they get older. This does not mean that their asthma has gone away for good. There is no cure for asthma yet.

About one-third of children with asthma will have symptoms as adults.

Asthma is a lifelong condition. With help from doctors and medicine, people with asthma can go into **remission**. People who start to have asthma later in life are less likely to go into remission.

KEY WORD

Remission: a period of time when the signs of an illness go away.

How Is Asthma Treated?

Asthma is **treated** in a few different ways. Some people are given pills. Most use inhalers. These are also called puffers. The medicine in a puffer opens up the airways so people with asthma can breathe better.

KEY WORD

Treated: given medical care.

There are two types of inhalers. One inhaler is used if you need fast relief from a bad asthma episode. Another kind of inhaler is used every day to keep symptoms under control. Many people use both kinds of inhalers. Quick-relief inhalers are often blue.

Asking for Help

If you think you might have asthma, ask an adult to find you a doctor. Getting help in time is very important when you have an asthma attack. Here are some conversation starters.

"I can't breathe now. Can you get my inhaler?"

"I have asthma. Smoke is my trigger. Can you take me somewhere else?"

"I'm worried that I might have an asthma attack. Can you find some help?"

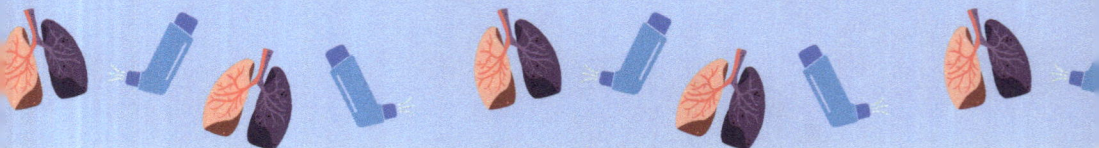

How to Help Someone Who Has Asthma

If someone you know is having an asthma episode, it is important to help them right away. Here are some ways to offer help.

Find their inhaler

If someone you know is having an asthma episode, ask them where their inhaler is. Help them find it and use it.

Move them away from triggers

If you know what has triggered their asthma, get them as far away from the trigger as you safely can.

Stay calm

Try to help them stay calm. Panic makes asthma worse. Sit them upright. Lying down makes it harder to breathe. Find an adult to help you if needed.

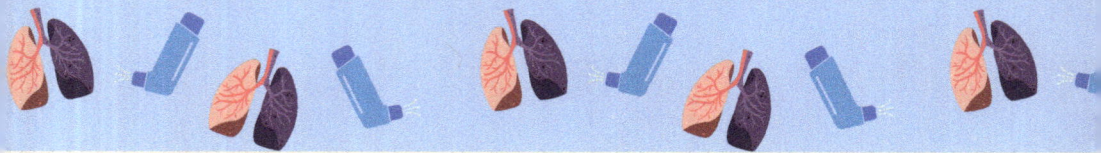

the History of Asthma

Hippocrates was a Greek physician who lived more than 2,000 years ago. He was the first person to link breathing problems to triggers. The word "asthma" is Greek for short of breath.

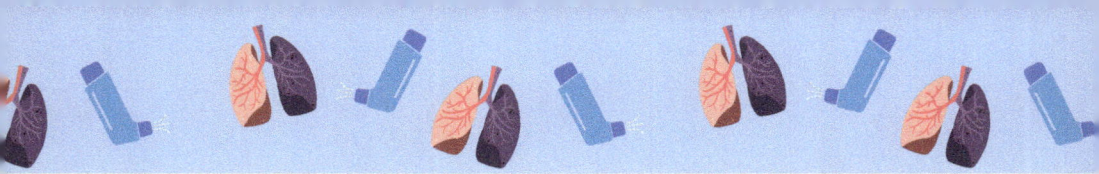

A scientist named Irving Porush created the modern inhaler. It went on sale in 1957. Since then, it has changed people's lives.

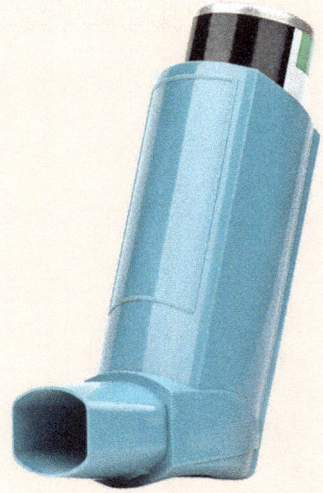

Asthma Superheroes

Some people choose to talk openly about their asthma. Others do not. Everyone has to figure out what works for them. Here are some asthma superheroes who are happy to share their experiences.

Singer **Pink** has had asthma since she was two years old. That has not stopped her from putting on exciting shows. She does not often need an inhaler. Her asthma was triggered when she had COVID-19.

Jerome Bettis played football for 13 years. He took medication for his asthma before every game. He is living proof that having asthma does not need to get in the way of being a top athlete.

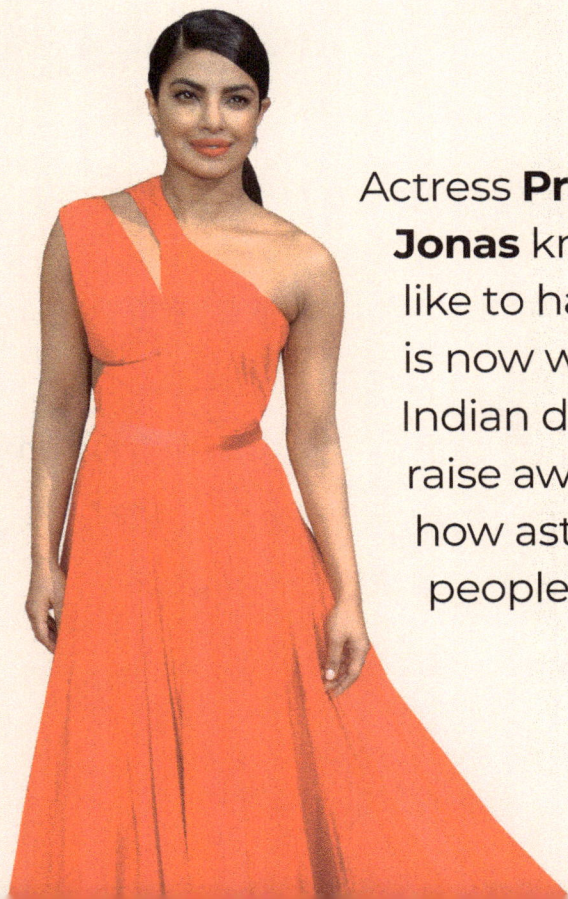

Actress **Priyanka Chopra Jonas** knows what it is like to have asthma. She is now working with an Indian drug company to raise awareness about how asthma affects people's lives.

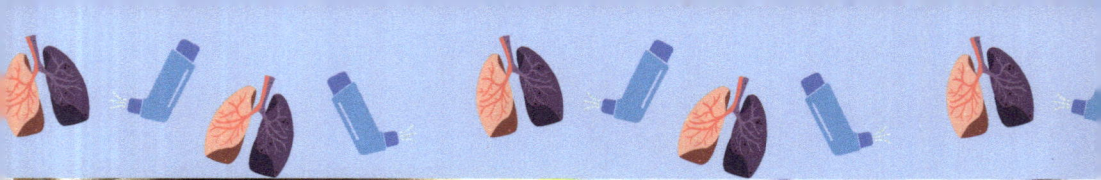

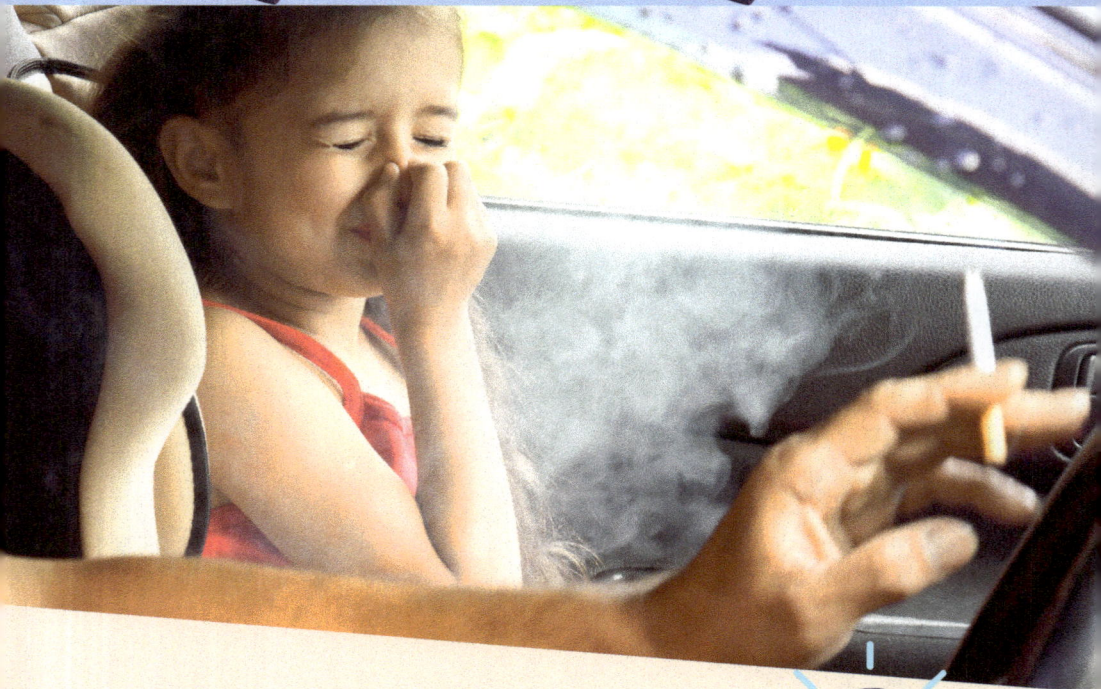

Asthma Tip 1: Noticing Your Triggers

Be aware of when you have asthma symptoms. Notice what might trigger the symptoms at those times. It might be something in the air or something you eat. It can also be something you do, such as exercising.

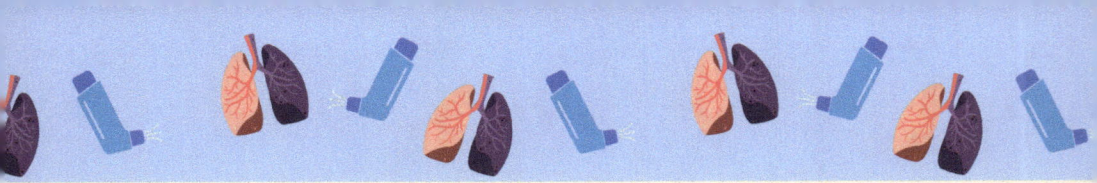

When you know your triggers, do your best to avoid them. Tell your parents, your friends, and other adults in your life what your triggers are. Ask them to remove the triggers or take you away from the triggers.

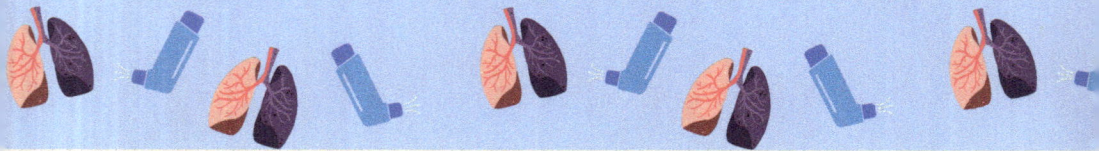

Asthma Tip 2: Creating an Asthma Action Plan

Your doctor may want you to make an Asthma Action Plan. It tells you and other people what to do when you have asthma symptoms or when you have an asthma episode. This is a good thing to carry with you at all times.

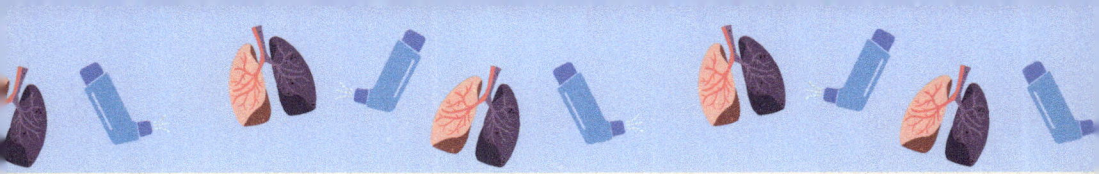

You can ask an adult to find an example online and help you make a plan. Your plan should include these:

1. Your name and your doctor's name

2. Who to call if your asthma is really bad

3. The inhalers you use and how and when to use them

4. A list of things that trigger your asthma

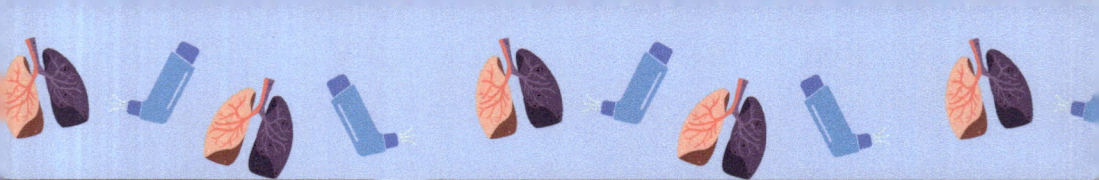

Asthma Tip 3: Practicing Self-Care

Asthma can make you feel tired or worried. You might want to be alone or you might want to be with other people. This is up to you. Try to do something that makes you feel better.

Some exercises will also help your asthma. Walking in nature, doing yoga, or swimming are some good options. Make sure you avoid exercises that might trigger your asthma.

Quiz

Test your knowledge of asthma by answering the following questions. The questions are based on what you have read in this book. The answers are listed on the bottom of the next page.

1 What is asthma?

2 What are some common triggers?

3 Can asthma symptoms come on fast?

4 What does the medicine in an inhaler do?

5 What is remission?

6 Who created the modern inhaler?

Explore Other Level 3 Readers.

Visit www.engagebooks.com/readers

Answers: 1. A condition that makes it hard to breathe 2. Pet hair, air pollution, pollen, cold air, and smoke 3. Yes 4. Opens up the airways 5. A period of time when the signs of an illness go away 6. A scientist named Irving Porush

www.ingramcontent.com/pod-product-compliance
Lightning Source LLC
Chambersburg PA
CBHW051234020426
42331CB00016B/3370